The Decadent Book of Babylon

Michael Perret

Curious Corvid
PUBLISHING

The Decadent Book of Babylon by Michael Perret
© 2024, Michael Perret
All rights reserved.

Published in the United States by
Curious Corvid Publishing, LLC, Ohio.

First Printing Acknowledgments:
Orpheus & Eurydice (The Lovers Journal, Issue 2)
My Muse's Orgasm (The Erozine, Issue 5)
The Sad Bacchante (New Delta Review, Issue 12.2)

Cover Art by Louis Braquet
Formatted by Ravven White

ISBN: 978-1-959860-31-0

Printed in the United States of America
Curious Corvid Publishing, LLC
PO Box 204
Geneva, OH 44041

www.curiouscorvidpublishing.com

First Edition

Trigger Warnings

This work contains graphic depictions of violence including sexual assault, incest, and murder.

Table of Contents

After Sappho

The Orpheus Head

And with bronze they cut off his head and nailed it to his lyre
and threw them both into the Thracian sea…
And the grey waves carried them both to Lesbos.

Phanocles

Renée Vivien reclining on her fainting couch:

And write to Natalie, I must thank her
For the invitation to Glück's *Orphée*.
But tell her I'm dying — I can't save her
From Hades or her distractible eye —

You know that Orpheus used to be sung
By a castrated man. Now a woman,
A true daughter of Lesbos, sings that song —
That role — the Decapitated Patriarch
Of Song. It just fell into her lap — just
Came in with the tide and lapped at her feet —
Her inheritance, and mine, the washed up
Shipwreck of her paternity, and mine —
Apollo's lyre and the Orpheus head —

Remember when Heredia's daughter
Came with Pierre for *The Orpheus Head*?
Well, before the show he asked us if he
Could photograph us fucking — he called it
Modeling. I laughed, and let Marie in —
For him though Lesbos was forever closed

Marie and I talked about poetry
For a while. I said, "Your *Persephone*
Is beautiful. It strikes me as more true
Then your father's sonnets, but men are rough —
It takes a woman's touch to touch me —
                                        'Then

Opening your purple pomegranate
You pressed your lips into mine for so long
And the flavor of that moment was strong
And so sweet… that the seeds passed through your kiss
Changed me forever — '
                        My Eurydice's
Name is Violet. Persephone has her,
And I have the void. Play me, I resound —
I'm hooked on Persephone's little pills —
Her little capsules filled with emptiness —
Pop — pop — No, the gods are not kind."

                                        Atthis!
Here, send Cleis for more chloral — and Atthis,
Remember when we made love on the beach
And I sang that sacred Lesbian hymn
In praise of the virgin and the love void?

The poet lives for love and art alone
And this, Atthis, is how her body dies:

A hollowed-out instrument, and her chest
Echoing with emptiness when her breast
Fills with the song the sublime mourner sang —
When he cursed nature, the gods, when he rang

His own death knell—when he cried out her name
Again and again, the same name the same
Pain: *Eurydice!* I am that man's heir—
Daughter of the joined Sappho/Baudelaire—
I found poetry in French, but in Greek,
My mother tongue, at last, I learned to speak—

Eurydice, I will mourn you, the bride
Of the nature singer, and, when you died
And the sad hero failed to bring you back,
The virgin mother of the sun turned black.

The Orpheus Head

i. Orpheus in Hades

By these broken strings, this Orpheus head,
Cradle me, my song newborn from the sea—
Comfort me, hold me, I am the unwed
Widower. I pled—they ignored my plea:

Hades, your love for Persephone—*please*—
Remember how far for her you would go!
I have crossed the line that life itself flees
And yet my passion has not ceased to grow!

Persephone, goddess, still underground
There is life, bulbs and tubers, fertile roots—
Nature has always quickened to the sound

3

Of my song, and turned its tendrils and shoots

To me—You two, I believe, you can hear
The profound truth in my longing, and see
The depths of my grief, the cold in my fear,
The sense of the loss of Eurydice

To me...

ii. The Sirens

      I think I should have let them die—
The Argo, the whole wayward ship of fools—
For when the sirens started, so did I
To pour in false hopes, to stir the whirlpools

Already roiling inside of their chests—
For like Medea (who forsook her home
And followed her father's immoral guests
And dyed the crests red and thickened the foam

That frothed at the oars as, backs turned, we fled
Through her brother's blood) the things we had done
We too had done for Jason (we had bled
Blameless bystanders, abandoned hearts won—

Left Delians dead, Lemnians alone...)
When sunk in dark upon dark reflection,
Suddenly I felt the ship's senses hone—
Every man tensed in every direction—

The waves seemed muted, sound itself seemed still —
Then out of the lull, voices, soft at first,
Reached our ears, we looked — but then they turned shrill,
And only then did I discern the worst —

I grabbed Tiphys's arm, threw him back, strummed
The lyre and like thunder echoed the dome —
The ship's deck, quick with Thracian rhythms, drummed
As my voice came, like a plow through the loam,

Snaking in slowly, a heavy, low drone,
Singing, O goddess, a song that you know
About a love not so unlike your own:
Cadmus and Harmony's descent below

As serpents…

iii. Cadmus and Harmony

For, I sang to those men, *when*
He sowed the teeth of the dragon he slew
To found a city for Apollo, men,
Each one an Ares, from the soil grew —

And they would have killed him, but like Jason,
He threw stones in their midst, and so they fought
Each other, and Cadmus, the great mason
Of Thebes, founded the city he had sought —

5

And the gods seemed pleased when there in his hand
There appeared what he felt was a flower,
But on its finger was a wedding band
And in its weight an immortal power —

Harmony's, given to him in marriage —
Then around them he heard music, saw lights
As each god came pulled in its own carriage —
Hymaneus with his torch led the rites…

When the sirens' voices were out of range
I stopped singing, for the danger had passed,
But the song of Cadmus pursued its strange
Aires in my head as I stared at the mast—

"Orpheus," Jason commanded me, "sing!
"Keep singing!" he ordered, but I was still.
The song itself was a dangerous thing—
Cadmus was blessed, but he'd cursed the gods' will.

In a trance the song to its last note played
Behind my eyes until Cadmus I saw
Full length, face down, in the mud as he prayed
"O gods, I can still smell its fetid maw—

The monster I slew for you, and can see
Its teeth, its multiple tongue, the abyss
Behind its throat, its gorge lined with debris
And hear the multiple roar of its hiss—

Mortals do these things to be more like you—

Make journeys, kill monsters, found cities, then
Endure unrest until, when they are through,
They look up and pray, again and again:

Make me immortal – in death make me shine!
Have I proven my worth, what else can I
Do – That is their last prayer, but now hear mine
As I look down, my back turned on the sky:

Make me *more* mortal, make more of me touch
The earth, then let me, my eyes turned away
From the shame of mankind acting too much
Like gods, die and into this earth decay – "

Then the spiteful transformation occurred!
As Cadmus was given just what he wished –
His bones melted, flesh coalesced, sight blurred –
In near darkness his tongue flicked, hissed and
swished –

Then laughter rained down from the heavens for
Aphrodite wanted to watch him writhe –
But Cadmus was not alone and before
She could stop what was happening, her lithe

And graceful daughter became just like him –
His mortal skin felt the immortal grasp
Of Harmony's hand, as she, limb by limb,
Went with him – But, oh! Aphrodite's gasp!

To see her become a thing of the ground!

7

She watched in disgust as her daughter changed
To join her husband — coiled around him — bound
To be forever from the gods estranged

In her renewal of her wedding vow…

iv. Eurydice

Is she here, goddess, did Harmony chase
His shade? I saw nothing from Charon's prow —
I so longed to see Eurydice's face —

"BEHOLD IT, SINGER, BEHOLD IT NOW!" Then
The shadows dissolved — the abysmal mass —
Into a sea of shades around us — men —
Women — my Eurydice! "LET HER PASS!"

The voice of the death-god intoned to them,
And slowly her steps led her back to me
Through dust and ashes and the soiled hem
Of her shroud — I wept — I thought we were free —

I thought Persephone had heard my song
For what it was, heard me and in a burst
Of sympathy blessed me — but I was wrong —
The blessings of the gods are always cursed —

"AS SIGHT AND COLOR RETURN FROM THE
BLACK
"YOU WILL FEEL HER WEIGHT COME IN IN
YOUR HAND,

"NOW GO," she forewarned, "BUT DO NOT LOOK
BACK
"OR HER SWELL WILL RECEDE AND TURN TO
SAND — "

v. The Death of Orpheus and the Birth of Sappho

Hold me, mother/daughter, take me inside!
I looked and Eurydice slipped away —
No – no – I whispered, and all the trees sighed
And mournfully echoed me in their sway —

With just enough light for an endless dusk
The creatures around me wanted to die —
I began to sing of an empty husk
And a void, a truth flung against a lie —

I cursed the death-god, his wife, her rebirth —
My words tongued Aphrodite like a cud —
Then I spit her out, the goddess of mirth,
And purged the rest in a blasphemous flood

That rocked Mount Parnassus, made it reverse —
The muses all clenched their bellies and moaned —
Life is death, love is loneliness, a curse –
My song repeated — repeated and droned —

I sang until my throat dried and I coughed
And coughed out the earth — and coughed out the
dust —
I was feared because when I sang I scoffed

At the womb too, and nature's trick, it's lust —

It made me crave her — awakened a thirst
For her kiss and called me — *Come, plant your seed* —
Then it betrayed me — last things were put first —
It took my heart, left an unfulfilled need,

And buried that instead: but inside me.
Inside this hollow instrument she came —
She filled me up with a hole, like a sea
In reverse, she discharged into my frame

Her song, her daughter, her black sun, her gift —
And when those murderous midwives arrived
And tore off my head and set it adrift
It was only for her that I survived

And Apollo's lyre — Here, take me inside
Now and with your fingers divine the chords,
Sing with your voice, with your genius divide
My stream into stanzas and guide me towards

The birth of poetry in Lesbos — Sing
Into being a new master and muse —
Her name will be Sappho — her art will bring
A new virgin race, untouched and unuse-d —

— Dika, where is Cleis, the pain is too much —
And turn off that music, please — I can't hear —
Keats said somewhere — the music in our heads —
The longing long-distance — love is better

In verse — Tell Natalie to take a hearse
I won't be able to save her tonight
I have to write —
                    I mean *writhe* —
                                        I mean *die* —

To Violet

I am the dead one – you still live in me –
The walls of an empty tower on fire
My lungs cough up smoke and my broken lyre
Clangs to your name and the other debris

That make up my songs to you and my plea
For new life, to die, and when I expire
To find, among the shades, you, my desire,
My true love, reborn, my Eurydice –

A flower, even in death's dark meadow,
I'd find her – I know all her hues and scents –
And if we end up in death's dank ghetto

Oh, there, at least, I won't feel your absence;
Still, like a vacuum pressed in through the skin
Where your touch should be, should have always been –

Orpheus and Eurydice

Orpheus, *after Nerval*

I am the shadow. Hollow is the tomb.
I am the prince. The tower burned alone.
My lute is made of stars. I am the lute.
I am the black sun. Melancholy, I—

I sing immortal. I sing without breath.
I breathe the still breath. I am death. It lives.
The night forever has fallen and still
In longing and in dreams I sing to her:

Everything I desire stays in fire still
There where I smolder on our wedding's eve
Your death is my desire made eternal

And still — I see you in a vision-lit
Day — dreamt in the mists off this restless night
Where I hopelessly become one in one —

Eurydice, *after Heredia*

Whoever you are, of the living, keep
Going, don't stop at my burial mound —
Don't crush the wildflowers on the ground —
I can hear the ants crawling — the vines creep —

Why are you stopping — I hear its soft cheep —
Don't offer it here — instead share the sound
Of birdwings in flight, they're like a soul bound
Light-wards — like a phoenix — up from the deep!

Once, from the grass we heard a serpent's hiss —
Then, lost in the shadows, I saw his form —
Two times I stood on the threshold of bliss —

Is the sun still pure joy — O, does it shine —
I felt it at the gates, present and warm —
I can still feel my husband's hand in mine —

after Sappho

He must be a man
With more confidence
Than I, who can still
Breathe close to your breath's
      fall

And bathe in the light
Like the day when you
Smile and your laughter
Disperses in the
      wind

I choke, and my tongue
Brakes, a trembling heart
At the brink sputters
The trembling holds me
      down

When by chance we meet
With a trembling heat
Quakes my every vein
And eyes wide I stare
      off

I grow pale with sweat
My ears trembling ring
I come to believe
It's me, that distant
      cloud

I mean, this distance
It feels like death, like
To talk to you would
Take Orpheus in
      song

Charming the forces
Of loneliness and
      long

Nights spent in silence —

Kept from myself and
      you

Song on a Theme from Sappho

I think I know why
Sappho was so nervous

She spent too much time
Fantasizing about

The person she loved
Before asking her out,

And writing her poems —
O Sappho, preserve us!

The beloved comes
Upon us too quickly

And we know, *Oh, no,*
She's the one, we are doomed…

To rapturous flights
Daydreams stopped, but resumed

A moment later
Looking pale and sickly

Our worried friends will
Ask, *Hey, what's the matter?*

But we won't confess
It, our silence and shame

They'll guess and demand
It, *Yes! Tell us her name!*

And this will just make
Us sadder and sadder

Until one day, lost
And shaking all over

We find her sitting
On a bench, and decide

To approach her…Our
Eyes meet — No — we can't hide —

We take our dreams and
The rhymes we wove her,

And —

Singular Duet

I've heard them described as missed connections —
But we were like two dead stars face to face
Reflections inspired by old projections
Black sun constellations drifting through space

Sirens, false beacons attracting the gaze
Into blind alleys, wrong turns, and lost time
Chimeras leading one into the maze
Of thoughts as in vain as they are sublime

We were for each other's eyes but a glance
Caught and cast in an eternal mold, still —
Statues, but in dreams, unable to dance
Empty chests, love voids, to, yes, *un-fulfill*

A paradox of parallel untouched
Dimensions, tragically glimpsed, when we met
Like ghosts, hands, through the mists, outstretched,
unclutched,
And fell into this singular duet...

Song

I thought of you again last night
    in the dark
The thought turned me on like a light
    in the dark

Remember how our glances met
    in silence
They seemed to speak of past lives, yet
    in silence

I thought I knew you but then, no,
    I didn't
Say something — but — knees shaking — so,
    I didn't

What was it that made me lose my —
    Was it your — ?
That caught me off guard before I —
    Was it your — ?

One day I'll say what I can't say
    in a poem
Pray for it, now that we don't pray,
    in a poem

An Orphic Song

My lover doesn't
Love me, but is it
      wrong

To mourn my lover's
Love with an Orphic
      song?

The Poet's love flared
When Eurydice
      died

Like a trick candle,
And so does mine, I've
      tried

To hide it, but, Look!
I see smoke in the
      air

So, like him I sing,
I signal and I
      bare

My heart, waiting for
The maenads to gore
      me

And with my lyre dump
Me, headfirst, in the
     sea

Song

My heart is broken —
                it's a broken thing…
Now there is nothing
                for me but to bring
it's random pieces
                back here and to sing
sad songs to soften
                and to numb the sting…

The Sad Bacchante, *after Renée Vivien*

Now done with the arrogant rays of day
Penetrating the woods of enchanted nights,
It is the hour when the Bacchantes sway
To languid rhythms and dance in their rites.

Their tangled hair weeps the blood of the vines,
Their feet are fast, light, like wings on the wind,
Their bodies are pink and their supple lines
Like smiles fill the forest from end to end.

The song of the youngest, more like a cry,
Struggles up her throat; it's swollen, it throbs.
Unlike the others, she's pale, she could die
From the bitterness, from the swell of sobs.

Preserved in its wine, the harvest sun still glows,
But she's helpless, she can't forget her pain.
She's still half-drunk but her drunkenness *knows*…
A wreath decorates her brow, but in vain.

She's tired of fake joys, of false addresses;
The thought of the cold, hard morning after
Corrupts their hot and honeyed caresses.
Pensive, among the roses and laughter,

She doesn't know desire without regret,
The one on her back but always aware;

She remembers the kisses you forget
And the flowers crushed by the orgies there —

Yes, in a dream I slept with the daughter of Cyprus, *after Renée Vivien after Sappho*

Yes, I possessed you, O daughter of Cyprus!
Pale, I serviced your voluptuous desires...
I had you in the torchlight of Hesperus,
    Your immortal body.

And my flesh came to know your star-flesh it
craves...
And I embraced the flame, the shadow, the dew,
And your moans died away like the breaking waves,
    Lustful — crashing — through.

A mortal, I drank from the cup of the gods,
I parted the rippling azure of your robes...
My caresses made your eyes agonize... Your
    Bed reflected stars...

Since then, in Lesbos, the night calls me in vain,
In vain, the sapphic harps resonate their gold...
Yes, I possessed you, O daughter of Cyprus!
    In my dream of ardor —

Prayer to Aphrodite

Cyprian girl with the flashing eyes,
Goddess of love at first sight, gently
Fill her heart with bittersweet surprise
    And make her love me

Appendix:

Love Void, *Fragments from Earlier Works*

I.

Suddenly seeing that you weren't there
did falling in love
did falling in love with you
did falling in love leave the moment empty
would not loving you now leave the moment empty

before you, now — nowhere
without you, now — nowhere
nowhere is somewhere
where

between desire and despair
where do I stand

II.

I think
behind the fear

beyond the fear
she is

I think
behind the trembling frame
the silent stutters
the blank face aflame
the surface eyes away

beyond this
she is

and I am

immersed
in real time

a time-
state

of touch
and be

touched

a future

III.

The sun comes up
I long for you
The sun goes down
I long for you

I long for you
in the moonlight

still longing

IV.

My heart
pumps
void

pumps
hard
hollow
void

in a chest
like a stomach

starved

V.

hiding, heart banging
in the chest to be

heard, but it is not—
seen, but it is not—
      known

and I in secret

VI.

Muses, stay away –
Let my master's song
Be sung – his daughter
And all of hers shall
        sing

Orpheus *alone –*
As he sang, alone –
Married to a life
Undone, and made to
        live

On and on, longing –
On in ever loss –
For his song begins
Love, *and unends* love-
        void

Sirens Still Burning

I.

We were burning

Like collapsed stars in time

II.

We were burning
collapsed stars in time

burning

burning hopeless burning

futilely burning in time

like stars collapsed
outside of time burning

a scene at a distance

time aflame in empty space

a flame

burning

nothing

III.

We were burning
like collapsed stars in time

burning

a sinking ship burning

A beacon in the mist —

a beacon

burning

nothing

IV.

We were burning
collapsed stars in time

burning

futilely burning

futilely burning

futilely burning in time

like cores collapsed
outside of time

burning

we were burning
we were burning

cores collapsed

outside of time burning

futilely burning in time

V.

A sinking ship
burning

a collapsed star

a beacon burning
in the mist

a flame

A flame!

Look –

then

Listen –

VI.

A sinking ship

burning

time itself burning

a beacon

aflame

and

outside of time burning

eyes that mirror flames

hands that grip

and

hands that slip

eyes that sink

and

eyes that cease

VII.

Eyes that cease

to burn

The Decadent Book of Babylon

The Rape of Derketo

1. Incantation to Sappho in Hades

Underground in Hades, in perfect night,
Do you recall your island, O Sappho?
The orchards your lyre sang into tableaux
Of apple blossoms, fresh, soft pink and white?

You who were both lover and the one loved,
Do you recall Atthis, her pale shade
Laughing, demurring, napping in the glade
Of myrtles, virginal, even when shoved?

Do you recall the tripods and the flames?
And in the night, Eranna's voice chanting,
Her breath like wings or animals panting
At their games, her lips pressed with sacred names?

Your mouth is music, open it— Answer!
Do you recall your home in Mytilene?
Joyful cries were heard there, full kisses seen!
That place where you were both queen and dancer!

See the sea again, the coast to the east,
Not that far in the violet, setting sun,
And compose a song, each verse, one by one,
Perfect, but on barbaric airs released…

2. Sappho Presiding over Orphic Rites of Initiation in Hades

Inheritor of the lyre and the wrongs
Lamented in the mysteries and prayers,
The sacred rites, the impossible pairs
Entwined to spite Aphrodite, the songs

Of Orpheus, the first hymn to be sung
When a new girl, the initiate, brings
Her voice to the chords, her touch to the strings,
Darkly lit by the candle's flaming tongue

Is to Derketo. It is what I sang,
Naked, before my sisters, lovers, friends —
All of whom, having met their mortal ends,
Are with me here. Living memories hang

All around us like mirrors. Sisters, kneel
Before your beloved, and as these notes
Saturate your spirits and parch your throats
With longing to sing, take her and feel

3. Derketo at Aphrodite's Bath

Yourself taken by an ancient desire,
The same that made Derketo shake and burn
At the baths when she'd hesitate to turn
Her head to look, to stare, or to admire

Too strongly Aphrodite's perfect form,
Indifferent, in the grotto's clear waters
Washed by nymphs, anointed by her daughters;
And Derketo at sea, lost in a storm…

Her trembling hand, her anonymous touch,
Having brushed and pressed the goddess's breast,
Withdrawn and longing to explore the rest,
But certain she'd gone too far, done too much,

Exposed her heart to her goddess's wrath,
Wishing she could die, submerged in the source
With Aphrodite's used oils, her remorse
Coiling, breathlessly, in one final bath —

4. Derketo Loves Love's Goddess

"Derketo! Wake up! The goddess wants you."
"Wants me?" — "Yes, and when you're finished, I
heard
Satyrs are coming! The whole reckless herd!
Try to be here when they come splashing through!"

Her sister smiled, dove in, and swam away,
But Derketo knew she would *not* be back,
Pretending to flee them, flat on her back
Playing the role of satirical prey —

No! Derketo loves love's goddess — would burn
Eternally before she would submit

Again to the rut of the male, admit
That mortal thing inside her, let it churn

As though in soil, planting spoilt seeds of death –
Derketo loves love's goddess, and could live
Forever and never die, never give
Herself to the living, but transcending breath

Be one of the gods, Aphrodite's flame
Burning, on fire, unending, her coming,
The voice of her ecstasy, her humming
A song on her lips, her desire, her name –

5. Aphrodite Progenitrix

"Aphrodite," Derketo called, "I'm here!"
The overhanging trees began to brush
Their leaves together, and then in a rush
She saw the goddess of love reappear.

She looked like a woman, in form and shape,
Naked and rich as nature, and with child,
Attracting the vines and everything wild,
That teased at her feet and reached for her nape.

Derketo blushed and tried to hide her face.
"What is it nymph? Don't you like what you see?
The goddess of love? Don't you still want me?
Or in reality would you replace

This with your perverse fantasies and dreams?
Still this moment, grey out these shades of green,
Stop time, stop growth, kill this baby, demean
The meaning of love, *me*? So it seems…

You'd seduce me, trap me, make *love* your own,
Reduce me to an idol for your eyes,
While your fingers deceive you, and the lies
Your heart tells you turn me fast into stone,

A towering statue to the world's end,
Where a nymph believed the goddess loved her…"

6. Sappho Falters

My lips tightened — I felt my voice falter.
A girl embraced me, kneeling. *Thank you, friend.*

The song is almost over, but it's hard —
The gods are not merciful to traitors.
She was thrown into that heard of satyrs,
And I must sing how her body was scarred,

Marred, like a field sown with bulbs and thistles.
Though her eyes were dry, she let her wounds bleed
As she limped away, still dripping with seed,
Still followed by rude laughter and whistles.

7. The Birth of Semiramis

And making her way back towards the water
She planned to uproot herself by the womb,
Defy her sentence before it could bloom —
This was not her choice, her son or daughter.

She'd longed to transcend Nature into love —
She'd loved love's goddess, Aphrodite — She'd
Worshipped her — in private, longed to be freed
From the earthly — eyed the expanse above —

She'd loved a god, but the gods are not kind.
With satyrs, Aphrodite had raped her —
Entered and violently reshaped her —
Left her with child, like a fruit's thinning rind…

In the pool, she tried to cleanse her insides.
She pictured the seed as a speck of sand,
And wanted it out. She plunged in her hand —
But Aphrodite hates infanticides,

And matricides — she kept them both alive —
The baby would grow into a great queen,
Semiramis, decadent and obscene —
Aphrodite's doves nursed and made her thrive —

8. Derketo's Death and Afterlife

For Derketo, post-partum, sought out death,
And from a cliff cursed life, love, and the gods,
All lies, false promises, empty façades.
She'd believed in them, and with her last breath

She let out a scream, that fell as she fell.
Her scream is our Orphic song in the raw,
The ancient force that lends our art its awe-
Inspired power that no one can dispel —

10. Sappho in Eternity

The temple was quiet but for the breaths,
Devout and intimate, of all her friends…
And now, having found, all, their mortal ends,
Their shades continue, transcending their deaths,

To love in eternity in Hades…
Our love is no different, Sappho, still pure —
Unsoiled, our virginities still endure —
I sing *Renée* songs just for the ladies.

For Aphrodite still does our bidding
Since, mounting her chariot pulled by doves,
She heard your prayer for help winning your love's
Heart, though it was morally forbidding…

Because in the chest of another girl…
Nothing would come of your loves together,
No newborn child to act as a tether,
Pure love the one thing our flag lets unfurl!

Conquering the goddess who once had cursed
Derketo for loving her in that way…
Now, like Hades in Orpheus's sway,
She finds her will bound and her hands coerced

By your perfect music, the expression
Of the bittersweet that troubles desire.
That lyric, accompanied by a choir
Of voices, of calls for intercession

On behalf of love, now resounds throughout —
And Aphrodite, at our beck and call,
Defenseless before what you taught us all,
Answers every prayer that's true and devout —

The Decadent Songs of Semiramis,
Tableaux Vivants

Introduction

Natalie:

In decadent times, those women are free
Who have means to create a private sphere,
Where their sisters can be themselves and fear
Nothing—Sisters, welcome. The others, see

That you do not offend Pauline and me—
Don't try to sneak in, like a Trojan steer,
Seedlings from your wooden cock and balls. Here,
Defeated and tamed, Aphrodite, she

Serves only us, answers only our prayers,
Demands nothing of us for our affairs,
Keeps our licentious virginities clean—

But if our walls were breeched from the outside,
Like Babylon, they would be purified
By fire!—See for yourself, behind this screen:

The Death of Sardanapalus, *tableau vivant 1*

Sardanapalus:

No, not yet! Find my poet! Drag her in!
Myrrha, poetess, listen to this din!

Babylon's last cries, and I, of her whores,
The very last—I need you!—Block the doors!—

I need you to sing while Babylon burns,
While Babylon laughs and Babylon spurns
Nature, now and as she always has, for
Even as we speak, the Whore's children pour
Holy oils onto Her pyres, prepared
To throw their own bodies, exposed and bared,
Into the flames! I have ordered total
Immolation, from the sacerdotal
To the slave—horse to sacrificial bird—
An absolute end—I've given the word—
Nothing left!—No!—not the hint of perfume—
For the god or for the flood to consume!

For Aphrodite's once again fertile—
The river's free, it waters the myrtle—
It undermines impenetrable walls—
The decadent end to decadence calls—

The ancient prophecy has come to pass:
When the river fills, when the floods surpass,
Then nature, laid siege to your present will
Take it, and in it a future instill.
Not in my present! Gather it all up!
Every jewel, in the pyre! Every cup!
Every person living—Dig up the dead!
Burn it all! Melt it all! Flesh, bone, gold, lead!
All of it gone—The shrouds, the silk sashes!
The goddess gets smoke, the river: ashes!

Mud for one, for the other burning eyes!

Come poet, sing to this chorus of cries!
Sing of our founder, then down to the end
As far as you can until the flames rend,
Mid-verse, your voice from your throat, and you
choke
On our acrid essence passed into smoke!

Babylon's Last Poet, *tableau vivant 2*

Myrrha:

A lover and a poet, always I
Have lived for those two things: love and art — My
Lovers are all here — They're ready to burn —
Some are fucking, some lamenting this turn
Of fate — Who could guess the end of the world —
Our garden of delights, our orgy, hurled
Into the flames to avoid being drowned —
Now, I will mingle a decadent sound
In with the cries and the moans at this pyre —
The songs of Semiramis on my lyre:

A Herdsman Finds the Babe Semiramis,
tableau vivant 3

The quiet hour of a peaceful day
A herdsman returns from checking his herds
His step is slow, his mind wanders away
But comes back when he hears a flock of birds

He hears their coos, he hears their wings beating
He also hears — he thinks — another sound —
Is it a cub...? A calf or goat bleating?
One of his gone astray? He looks around

What is this? He waves his arms, and the birds
Scatter revealing a child in the reeds
Its eyes are bright, its babbling almost words
The herdsman is dazzled, fearful, proceeds

To pick her up — But how can this be? She's
So beautiful — She must be a god's child...
Aphrodite's, dear herdsman, and that breeze?
Sent to her daughter, exposed in the wild.

The Rape of the Herdsman, *tableau vivant 4*

Her adoptive father was terrified
When he woke one morning with her astride
His bucking body trying hard to hide

His desire, already deep inside her
Unable to stop, slow down, in a blur
Of immense rising, in his ears the whir

Of horse-power — He'd fall! — He was sure! — He
Held onto her driving hips until she
Leapt off of him as he came, his cock free

To shoot its mortal essence in the air
Like the hopeless cry of a rescue flare
Sent up from the earth but lost in the glare

Of the rising sun — His daughter's hair flew
Behind her like a banner whipping through
The sky as she streaked outside, came into

The day as though it were hers to do what-
Ever she wanted to do with it, strut
Her favorite horse around, even glut

Her lust on its silken, smooth chestnut coat —
She mounted it — a neigh caught in its throat —
And raced until she was far and remote —
Dreaming she was powerful and of note —

The Rise of Semiramis, *tableau vivant 5*

The herdsman wept when Semiramis left —
Left with an officer — left him bereft —

He refused to eat, until he found drink,
Where he'd drown his longing, and watch it sink...

The officer who took her for his wife
Believed he had met the love of his life

She'd join him on his campaigns as a man,
Dressed as a soldier, but she had a plan —

When she left him for another he cried —
When his tears ran out, there was suicide…

The other man was the king in his tent,
Impressed by the young soldier and content

To meet him in private… His fate was sealed —
When she dropped her armor, he gasped, then
kneeled…

The Conspiracy Against King Ninus: Semiramis and Ninyus, *tableau vivant 6*

"When the King retires," Semiramis said,
"I will go to him dressed like you instead
Of the uniforms he likes me to wear —
He might know it's me, but the guards will swear
It was you, come to speak to your father.
Don't worry, Ninyus, I won't bother
With explanations: I'll insert the knife.
He won't even realize it was his wife
Who betrayed him! Then you will claim the deed,
Abdicate and bestow the gift I need
To feel free to love you to the extent
I want… I need power to feel content
In my body — Then, you will know pleasure…
Forbidden things, delights beyond measure —
Forgotten things, ecstasies unconceived —
In power I'll undeceive the deceived,
And introduce new things, you at my side.
All you have to do is sneak in and hide

Under the bed. When the deed is done, we
Will leave together, and when they all see
Us, arm in arm, they'll forget their old king!
And when I show them what my reign will bring
Of decadent things, they will start to sing
Of me! Sing! and never cease their singing!"

Semiramis with Child, *tableau vivant 7*

Evil is made without effort. Nature
Does it. The Good is always the product
Of art — Who said that? Never mind — I'm with
Child — By the son? By the father? Unclear —
They're both dead, and the harem's filled with girls
Now — Girls and other unnatural things —
But Nature has found me; like Derketo,
Punished — Legend has it, despite the doves,
That Derketo was, in fact, my mother…
That Aphrodite raped her with a man,
Or a satyr, some say an entire
Herd — Why? Because she fell in love with love,
And longed to uproot love from dirt and soil…
How romantic. No, here decadence reigns —
Perhaps I am part satyr and was raped
Into existence for the god of love —
I don't particularly want this child.
I know! I'll leave it exposed in the wild.
Let Nature and Aphrodite nurse it.
We'll meet again if they preserve it and
Then I might have an heir who deserves it.

Semiramis Over the Corpse of Ara the Beautiful, *Tableau vivant 8*

rumor dangled before my mind
    your body, perfect and divine.
my best artists I sent to find
    and bring it to me line by line.

but it's never enough, that porn
    for the eyes. no, I needed more.
the touch and the smell of your worn
    foot, my hands around the contour

of your calf, of your thing, of your —
    that's the real reason I declared —
not on your country, on *you* — war!
    desire raged and I despaired

of every satisfying my
    senses with the beauty I longed
for — when you refused to reply
    to my open letters I thronged

through your gates, a sea of armed men
    with orders to carry you back
on its tide — I waited, but then
    when they brought you, I put on black...

cold and hard and devoid of breath,
    flaunting a self-inflicted wound...
I would not be denied by death

and had you brought to me cocooned

in blue velvet, to be unwrapped
    like a peace offering, in my room —
trembling I undid the folds, rapt
    to be in this decadent tomb

alone with your body — I slid
    one leg over and got astride
you — you were cold but hard — I did
    what I wanted with you inside

me — I'm glad you're dead — I don't need
    an heir and this was my first time
fucking a corpse…and with this deed,
    I fear nothing, there is no crime

I wouldn't commit — there are no
    limits to what I may do — live
forever, never die, and know
    all the pleasures life has to give —

Canto: Babylon's Son

A vicio di lussuria fu sì rotta,
Che libito fé licito in sua legge,
Per tòrre il biasmo in che era condotta.
Ell'è Semiramìs....[1]

I'm less myself than I am my mother —
Whore of Babylon, erotic self-slave —
I took her place here, but lost my other

Place in the world — Now, depraved, I deprave.
This city is my only time and place:
Today, I take what yesterday I gave.

Tomorrow, so that a slave can embrace
Me from behind, I'll order him: *Be free*
With my ass! Be merciless, and debase

Your ruling body!... Such is the degree
Of debauchery and decadence here.
My mother would be pleased. She exposed me.

I was found by a drunken herdsman near
A pond where, legend says, Derketo drowned
Herself. He loved me, but I came to fear

---

[1] "Her vice of lust became so customary that she made license licit in her laws to free her from the scandal she had caused. She is Semiramis..." Dante, *The Divine Comedy*, Canto V, lines 55-58 (tr. Mandelbaum)

His love when, drunk at night, he'd come around
Whispering that I reminded him of *her*.
His mind was rattled, his judgment unsound —

The crimes he committed on me still were
Illicit at the time... They're legal now.
So, I ran. What followed that is a blur,

But things became clearer when I saw burn
A small effigy of Babylon's queen,
And heard about Ninus, his heir's return...

They promised us food, a bed that was clean,
In exchange, we'd hear what they had to say.
We were led into a room with a screen.

The meal would come after, so we would stay.
Tired and suspicious, we were all wary
When, the candles snuffed, a light, bright as day,

Lit up the screen and we watched a merry
Herdsman discover a babe in the reeds.
My eyes widened as I watched him carry

The foundling into *my* childhood home — Beads
Of sweat formed on my forehead as I watched,
Expecting to see the herdsman's misdeeds,

Perpetrated on me, on my soul notched —
But this story was different, not quite mine:
The child was a girl, the herdsman's plans scotched

When someone took her and left him to pine.
(He'd take it out on me till I escaped.)
Now, I watched closely and tried to divine

The identity of the one who'd raped
Him, avenging me, before I was born,
Creating the monster, the man reshaped,

Who'd love her through me, who'd use me to mourn
His loss — Now, I watched as she won a war
For a king she seduced, earning the scorn

Of her husband who, calling her a whore,
Killed himself, cheating himself of the fun
Of seeing her betray the king before

Getting rid of her accomplice, his son,
Only to find herself enthroned, with child…
Semiramis, the one and only one!

She exposed it to its fate in the wild.
And as I reeled at its–my bizarre fate,
They relit the candles and the reviled

Queen disappeared. There was more to relate
Though, and an old priest stood up: *I was there…*
I was there when the king was murdered late

In the night, ambushed by her, unaware
Of the corruption he had invited
In. I was there when, his son, in despair,

Questioned whether his love was requited.
For the throne he'd abdicated was filled
With promiscuity, while he, slighted,

Waited in the shadows…where he was killed
When his sighs became too tiresome and loud.
I was there when her water broke and spilled

Down the chest of one her slaves, who bowed
And was dismissed — This was in the throne room.
I was excited and already proud

Of our heir, and swore, once free from that womb,
I would care for it, cultivate its rule
Like new life resurrected from the tomb

She'd buried us in, as though in a pool
Of bodily fluids and perfume plunged!
I could breathe again — almost — Like a fool

I ran to her, spoke encouragements, sponged
The sweat from her brown, the wet from her thighs.
When he came out, instinctively I lunged

For him — I feared for his safety, his cries
Tore my soul with sympathy, hope and joy!
I would feed him the truth in this house of lies —

But before I could even touch the boy,
Not knowing to what immediate end,
He was taken, and discerning my ploy

To save the kingdom somehow: "Apprehend
"That priest," I heard Semiramis command.
"And expose the baby! As for him, send–"

My fate was on her lips, when with her hand
She touched her brow, lost consciousness, and fell
Back… I was imprisoned and later banned –

"Take me, then, to the city gates! Expel
"Me, liberate me from this wicked hole!"
I cried… but came back… Exile could not quell

My longing to see, free from her control,
My Nineveh, my home, once again good.
I've dedicated my life to that goal,

Found likeminded men, formed a brotherhood –
We're committed to finding our lost prince,
Exposed by the queen, for only he could

Take back the reins of this wayward horse since
The Whore of Babylon came self-proclaimed.
Only he can reverse our course, convince

The people that this decadence has lamed
Them, their future to a languid present
Lost, make them recognize her who has shamed

Them – We believe he is close, his ascent
Certain once we find him and lift him up –
We invite you to share in this event.

Impart what you know and, after we sup,
Stay — Join our struggle, we always need men —
Through this corrupt present, we'll raise a cup

Together to the future — And that's when
I stood up, for I'd realized who I was.
They recognized *her* face in mine, and then

Bowed, but nervously and confused because
They'd expected to see in my face *his*.
Nature has no respect for men, it does

What it likes — men have faith, but nature *is*.
That is the first blow to naive ideals…
Still the cause boiled, the effervescent fizz

Of my presence reigned over nightly meals,
Strategies were formulated and hatched,
Rumors were spread, packs were made, as were deals

Based on bribes — but we were not fairly matched.
Before we could even make our first move,
Whatever advantage we had was snatched

Right out of our hands, for in what would prove
My doing and undoing, a new law
Was put into effect, meant to remove

Any threats from the future that she saw
Menacing Babylon's decadent age —
Children were that threat and she meant to claw

Them back. One, above all, needed a cage…
The law expressly legalized incest,
In effect inviting me to engage

My estranged mother. So, "at her request",
We conceived an assassination plot.
It involved my knife buried in her chest.

I'd reveal myself as the one she sought,
Meet her, kill her, hear the public applaud,
And, it being still more moral than not,

Rescind all her laws, dissolve the façade
Of immorality, tear up and scrap
Her lascivious rule — But it was flawed

From the outset, our plan, our backwards map.
Whatever it took to get me inside
— Be it conspiracy or naïve trap —

Her again, that was *her* plan. When I tried
To approach her, on her throne, with my knife,
The guards pounced — but she ordered them outside.

Then she said, "If you mean to take my life,
I prefer you take it one on one. Let's
Do it right." Then she let her robes fall. "Strife

Is pleasure, especially when it gets…"
She moved towards me and now spoke up close,
"Intimate, intense, without safety nets…"

She brought my knife to her chest. *Grandiose*
Bitch, I tried to say, then she touched my cock
Through my robes. "You're free to, but why be gross

And make new holes when there's nothing to block
You from penetrating those that exist
Already—One of them you al-" — "You mock

Me…" My voice shook. "-ready—No, I insist."
With her hand she touched my cock to her sex,
And with one long leg wrapped around me, kissed

My lips, while I pushed into the vortex
Of her body, and as though being sucked
Into a void littered with all the wrecks

Of those who'd come before me and been fucked,
I came–back–into that womb, and was lost…
When I came to, I began to construct

My own Babylon on that holocaust
From which I came, born back on nauseous waves.
Her legs were spread, her chest gaped, she'd been
tossed

To the floor. I'd killed her and now her slaves
Were mine. I was the whore now. I'd driven
In my knife—How depravity depraves!

"More!" I screamed, and from crotch to heart riven,
I rolled in the mess of semen and blood.

I blessed the bequest I had been given

And added more ecstasy to the flood —

The Volcano Lovers

Part I. The Lesbians

L1

Suddenly she cries, "I feel the lips part,
A gorge open, an abyss — It's my heart —
A burning volcano — a deep void…
Nothing can comfort this monster you've
toyed
With or this fury's all-consuming thirst
Touched off by fingers like torches reversed
And raging in the fuel-pool of my blood!
When my passion erupts expect a flood!"

L2

Is that Baudelaire, Sappho, or the Marquis
De Sade?

L1

   Or maybe the heir to all three:
Me, in love and at this moment inspired
To sing to you until I am desired
Again.

L2

   Well, then *sing*, but let's take it slow.
I'm not ready yet for your volcano.
Read to me, or sing me a quiet song.
Quiet…but dirty — a *little bit* wrong.

L1

Then?

L2

          Then we can descend again, I swear,
Into the flames, the explosions we bear
Inside us—

L1

           We'll bathe, we'll swim in them, turn
Around and around, dance, incite and burn!

L2

I suspect you have been reading de Sade…

L1

Behind the sex, murder, the cursing God,
The long, very long lectures on French thought,
A romantic gesture, that one should not
Overlook, comes through…like a volcano.

L2

Groan!

L1

          But it's true! Every page is aglow
With it! It turns me on—it leaves me pale—
It's simply that Sade's Nature is female.

L2

La Divine *Marquise*.

L1

              Precisely and
All the libertines covet her right hand—
A place of honor held only by him,
Impatient to indulge her every whim
With his imagination and his quill.
Trust me, and I'll read you something that will
Tantalize your mind if not roil your heart.
In this scene no one dies. It forms a part

Of the last book of Juliette. Book six.
In her voice: *In Venice now, turning tricks*
For money and pleasure at a brothel
We own since our libertine betrothal,
My partner and I, the most immoral
Sluts with the most extreme bond, sororal
Connection, whatever, I won't say love.
My ass fits her freakish clit like a glove.

L2

Freakish clit…?

L1

              Sade writes, in Juliette's voice
And then his own: I believe Nature's choice
Is the tribade, the lesbian. They boast
Imaginations. What She misses most.
Imaginations that girls like us have.
Other women who fuck only to calve
Bore Her. To his mind She's totally queer,
And we are diverse, non-binary, near
To the monsters, the perverse, the ideal,
The multiplicity, the only real!
The Chimera, the Hydra, Medusa's snakes —

L2

But I only love women. The earth quakes
And I want you — binary — *not* a man.

L1

I know, but philosophically one can
Find room in Nature for all. In a footnote
Sade praises and defends just our kind. Quote:
"These charming creatures that idiots slur
So stupidly, on our culture confer

The same qualities they bring to pleasure:
They're friendly, quick, wry, in equal measure,
They're imaginative, talented, grace
In excess. Why fault them for an embrace
That belongs to Nature? Adversary!
Slow sectarian of ordinary
Pleasures, you condemn them because they
spurn
Your pious advances, but when we turn
To those willing to accept them, on par,
They're often almost as dull as you are!"

L2

How thoughtful. Did he really say those
things?

L1

Yes he did. And no one dies and he brings
No men into the scene they're attached to.
Juliette again: But I have to tell
You about this crazy party as well,
When four venetian ladies rented me
For the day. They waited for a stormy
Day — picked me up in a gondola — ooo-
La-la — just as the lightning crisscrossed
through
The sky — We reach the open sea — The storm
Breaks, the thunder makes itself heard — They
swarm
At me, the horny bitches! — One slut screams,
"Now's the moment!" — Another one
blasphemes,
"Fondle — Finger her! Everyone lick! Suck!

Come in defiance of the lightning! Fuck
You, chimerical God, who claims to make
Clouds crash into each other, the earth quake!
It's only Nature, and we don't fear Her!"
Oh my god, I was so turned on! The spur
Of blasphemy, the storm, their fingers, lips —
Waves splash our tongues, desperate hands
lose their grips,
Grab, caress, find another — The boat's tossed,
Lightning's striking everywhere — We exhaust
Every last orgasm, raging against
All that exists but our pleasure —!

                            Condensed
Thus into my verse translation! You look...
Tense?

L2

         One scene can't save an entire book,
Misogyny dripping off every page!
Just the thought cools me off — fills me with
rage —
Now that your author's sapphic rainstorm's
blown
Over, wet and hard *as a pumice stone,*
Here I am.

L1

            There's steam coming from your ears
Too.

75

Part II. The Volcano Lovers

L2

> Ugh! Just fuck your male gaze
> gondoliers!
> Maybe he's queer, but I'm a woman first!

L1

> I know — You're right — And he's one of the
> worst:
> "I use women for my pleasure, but I
> Despise them, and they disgust me. When my
> Fervid lust is satisfied, then I plot
> Against them. Disliked, sacrificed: the lot
> Of women." From *The Story of Jerome.*

L2

> And you dare to quote that pig in our home?
> And expect me to sleep with you again?

L1

> I do, for I'm plotting against those men
> Even as I quote them, author and part —
> Sade will be corrected, Jerome, my art
> Will turn into a woman, played by me.
> And you will play my valet, or lackey.
> We'll tour Mt. Etna, yes, the volcano,
> And meet a misogynist, who we'll throw —
> Wait — I'm getting ahead of myself — (*IN!*) —
> But enough of this prologue, let's begin:

The Volcano Lovers, or
the Madness of Dr. Almani

One day, exploring Mt. Etna, her womb
Vomiting flames, I stood before its spume
Of fire, and longed to be it, crying out,
And finding words and beginning to shout,
As I undid the buttons of my shirt,
And unhid my breasts, my man's belt ungirt,
"Headless pyramid! If I cannot be
The volcano, here, inside this body…
The destruction I feel raging inside
That, if I were me, would down this hillside
Flow on forever, engulfing these towns,
Because in my daydream the whole world
drowns,
The rest of Sicily and on and on…
If I can't be you then spit your flames on
This body, exposed to your spray of pain!"
Just then I heard a pistol's cock. —"What gain
Is there in executing a friend?" I
Turned, tightly holding my clothes to hide my
Body, and saw my valet with her gun
Pressed against a man's temple. *"There's*
someone
I can get along with," he continued.
My valet forced his head down. "Now, now,
you'd
Be wise to hear me out. I heard you, out-
Side of yourself with desire—" With the snout
Of her pistol, she forced him to the ground.

— "Quiet!" she yelled. "I heard something, and found
Him spying on you." — "Do you know me, sir?"
— "Like my own self, seen through the guise of *Her*,"
He answered, his face pinned down in the dirt.
— "And who is *She*?" I asked, fixing my shirt.
— "Nature, of course — Atrocious Nature —
That!"
Indicating Mt. Etna. Then he spat
Some dust, "who creates only to destroy."
— "Is he armed? Let him up, and let's enjoy
His 'friendship', at least for a little while."
— "Thank you," he said. "I do enjoy the stress
Of violent threats, but I must confess
I am armed — with knowledge," he tapped his head,
"If not the means at my fingertips. Led
By a scientific desire to know
Nature's secrets, I, a long time ago,
Begin to study the natural world.
As a chemist, its elements unfurled
Before me, I eventually came
To see that her sole, her principal aim
Is to cause harm to man — to you and me.
She is voracious, capricious, cruel. She
Creates for the sale of gross destruction.
And though, despite my thorough instruction,
I was not able to discern the cause,
Assiduous in my learning her laws,
I did invent techniques, and reproduced

Some of her effects…like those that induced
You to form, just now, a monstrous desire:
To drown the whole world in volcanic fire."
— "Do you mean to say, you can imitate
This volcano?" — "Indeed." — "And recreate
Eruptions? Earthquakes? Suffocating smoke?"
— "All of the above." — "Then it's time we
spoke
Of a demonstration and of the price
You demand for such knowledge." — "For
crime, vice,
Terroristic acts, I charge nothing. See,
The imitation of Nature leaves me
Thoroughly debauched." — "Sir, what is your
name?
I believe you are right — we are the same."
— "Dr. Almani. I am never wrong."
I smiled indulgently. — "Then come along…"
The sun was high and the air felt like breath
Exhaled by Typhon "…buried beyond death
In that volcano, some myths say."
— "Nonsense," Dr. Almani said. "The day
Is hot and we are in a cloud of steam —
Sulfuric steam — emitted from this seam
In the earth." We made our way to the shade
Of a small tree and sat. My valet stayed
Standing. He was thin, but with large features.
Grotesque, one of those carnival creatures
One encounters sometimes in works of art;
Unreal almost how well he played the part.
This was Dr. Almani when I asked

If he had really seen Nature unmasked,
And if he really believed that in fact
Nature was female. "No truth more exact
Was ever uttered." — "But aren't women
weak?"
I argued. "The weaker sex, all men speak
Of women so." I met my valet's eyes.
— "Indeed, but they only philosophize.
They are not scientists, like me. Besides,
Those God-fearing fools in love with their
brides,
Love to play at men with moral phrases
That mean nothing but the public praises.
The libertine's the true, unbiased man,
The individual who knows he can
Do what he wants if he's ruthless and not
Burdened by values that will get him caught,
Understands the female question this way:
Of women there isn't that much to say.
Women were created for our pleasure.
Their value, according to that measure,
Rises and falls, basically, at our will.
They're there to satisfy our whims until
Our desires change. And if they refuse,
Or if what we want is just to abuse
What little their bodies have to offer,
Torture and killing is what we proffer
To the threatened, the bored, the unfulfilled.
Dangerous animals need to be killed.
They harm us when they don't serve our
delights.

Enemies from that point on, our rights
As the stronger and the smarter require,
And have at all times and places where higher
Cultures predominate, the removal
Of your enemies. For his approval
On this point, read Machiavelli." — "Ha!"
I articulated, thinking *Bla-bla*
While imagining our "scientist's" fate.
"But She," I said, "the one you imitate,
In this contest, is she not the stronger?"
— "I can't keep it from you any longer!"
He smiled ruefully and stood up. "Let's go!
I want you to have what you want to know,
And like I said, I charge nothing for crime.
You want a demonstration? Well, it's time."
He led us to a tent we had not seen,
And began, immediately, to clean
A cannister on a makeshift table.
"Now, my friends, like I said, I am able —
But first — Welcome! My laboratory,"
He laughed. "Almost every category
Of her villainy I can reproduce.
The right materials, their proper use,
That's all that's needed." He spoke as he
worked,
And settling into his speech, he smirked,
Musing on Nature and himself at their
Worst. "My madness is just *her* heart laid bare.
The impulse to cause harm was, I believe,
Conceived inside me…" — "*Like women
conceive?*"

I joked, unheard. — "…through the profound
study
Of Nature, her viciousness, her bloody
Campaign of pure excessiveness, the Good
According to Her. Otherwise, why would
She create only to torment, destroy?
Disgust, terrify, distress and annoy?
Just cast a glance at the immensity
Of wrongs she scatters, her propensity
For evil, for deformities at birth,
Her monstrosities overrun the earth.
She never gives without adding some grief:
Science without popular disbelief,
Twelve hours of light, the same in darkness,
Richness, refulgence, then arid starkness,
Look, all these plants, but how many can kill?
Like lightning on a summer day. When will
People see that Nature is atrocious!
Love? Insane passion. Courage? Ferocious
Violence. Ambition? An amoral drive.
What animals have to do to survive!
Barely emerged from her profligate womb
Then it was crime, ignorance, or the tomb.
(Your instincts seem to have made the right
choice.
I could hear Nature calling in your voice
At the volcano's edge.) She swept me up
Immediately! Suckled at her cup
Of corruption, fed on all her horror,
I came to love it, though I abhor Her.
Yes, I'm her son, but I hate my mother."

—"I can see that." —"Of course you can,
brother.
Every scientist, every libertine,
Every atheist lives just to demean
Nature while imitating her effects,
And though my knowledge still has its defects,
...*What caused the dagger to be in her hand...?*
In a sense, I don't need to understand
Because I've caused, in whatever small way,
Her to be in mine, do my will, obey
My desires, though my desires are her wants —
Whore! Like those children of hers who have
cunts —
Voila! Captured in this jar and seething!
What shall we blow up? Whose guiltless
breathing
Shall we cut short? What about Sicily,
This beautiful island? Or Italy?
We'll terrorize the whole country entire!
Everything's good when excessive! Desire —
Look how hard I am just at the thought —!" —
"Not
Yet — Not yet — I myself just had a thought."
I winked at my valet. She was ready.
"What if that knowledge were there already,
The ultimate cause of why She is She?
You are right, we are the same, you and me,
But we're not her *sons*... No, we're her
daughters.
The answer why she creates and slaughters

Is in you. You are Nature — *female* — " —
"Sir…?"
We undid our shirts. "Him too? I mean,
her…?"
— "Her too. It's you," the pistol reappeared,
"Who needs to look again." And as we neared
The great volcano's rim, I explained,
"We are not killing *you*. What's to be gained
In executing a fellow witch?" — "What?"
— "You're confused, but behold this boiling
slut —
Is She not a mirror, does She not show
That so much of what you may think you
know
Is just metaphysics — old beliefs, lies?
Look! When the metaphysical male dies,
Suffocates and is burned inside this tomb,
You'll be reborn purified from this womb,
And your pieces like seeds will seminate
The next time She erupts to decimate
The surrounding country." — "Come on, sister!
Let me shoot him!" — "No, no, let him blister
In this volcanic heat. Not with your gun.
No, sister. I want to have some more fun
Before we throw him in. Tie his wrists! Lock
His legs! For once I wish I had a cock —
To come in a man's ass — What an affront
To procreation — expectations — !" (*grunt* —
Grunt) — "Keep your vulva, sister, the desire
To fuck without procreating's a dire
Warning to the world that we are our lust.

No, fuck him with your fist and use this dust
As cum, deep inside his fetid entrails —!"
We fucked him, threw him in. — "Look how he
flails!"
And fucked each other as Mt. Etna rent
Albani apart, until we were spent — "

Epilogue

L1

I'm breathless — Please tell me you're
breathless too —

L2

Yes! No — Chekhov's gun!

L1

What?

L2

It isn't
through!
The cannister. The jar. The bomb! Her heart
Laid bare.

L1

My god, who cares! It's only art!
Touch me — Hold me — Feel me trembling — My
fuse
Is a flick of your finger, or tongue — Use
Whatever you want —

L2

But I want to know!
Did they toss it into the volcano?

What? Did they blow up their parents'
chateau?
Did they use it to make more? Did they go
To the Vatican—?

L1

            Alright, alright—No—
That fictitious firecracker was so
Poorly—was so presumptuously made
That far from causing an earthquake it stayed
Perfectly still while letting out some smoke—
Man's attempt to master Nature a joke
Once again. There's only one way to reach
Those heights, those depths, words fail, they're
beyond speech;
There is no art, there's only what you know
When your body becomes *that* volcano,
In there, seething, humming, ready to come
To the surface where my touch—where my
thumb
Is pressing where my fingers want more—this

Is her heart laid bare—

L2

        Oh, Yes—

L1

           in a kiss—

Other Poems

Studies for a New Portrait of Myrrha, *first*

And when he asked her age, "The same," she said, "as Myrrha's."
Metamorphosis, Book X, Ovid (tr. Fitzgerald)

i.

The gods are cruel, but also, there are men.
Mama untouchable during the rites,
Father, finding himself free on those nights,
Wanted a girl. One of the gods was then

Sacrificed to during Ceres' time when
All prayers should have gone up to her. My rights
Were ignored. Led to his chamber, the lights
Were dim, but not dark. "Father—?" and again,

"Papa—?" but a god made him deaf, I guess,
Or twisted his ears, *No* sounding like *Yes*,
And though unbelievable, what I'd feared

The moment I entered and saw his eyes,
Whether they were filled with madness or lies,
Happened… I swear he saw me as he neared…

ii.

That god, Aphrodite, the cruelest one,
Ceres must have gone to her. I don't know,
But once he'd finished with me and was done
Undoing my future, I turned to go —

But then he said, in a voice that was low,
Harsh, "Myrrha." My name. I wanted to run,
But turned… What I saw was a volcano
Of stupid rage holding a sword — I spun

Back around, and ran — as far as I could —
I ran and ran, but I could always feel
Him there, somewhere, inescapably real —

So, I kept running till my legs, like wood,
Refused to bend — and, laying there, I heard
The sapling that, from his seed, in me stirred…

Studies for a New Portrait of Myrrha, *second*

I

i.

Desire is a prison, though, like a dream
It has wings and intoxicates like wine —
In flight you feel less human, more divine —
Eyes closed to cell walls, you feel the esteem

Of gods, and great men, who don't care and seem
Above it all — That's how it is with mine,
At least — Only an artist could design
Such an original passion and scheme

To keep me locked in it and self-deceived…
But such high-mindedness goes unbelieved
When, falling back, my eyes open and see

The ceiling of shame I was born to view
Like the inside of a coffin lid, you —
Your face engraved on it — staring at me.

ii.

Desire is a prison you're born into,
Carried and pushed and made to think your own.
You blame yourself when you're young. When you're grown,
You deny it was ever really you.

I don't blame you. I blame those men who grew
You, fed on the hints that they should have known
One day would produce a head like yours, grown
Up like Eve's apple, and just as taboo.

Myrrah, I tell myself. *Myrrah,* I say,
Remember, they made you. Blame them — but try
Not to fool yourself — No — Identify,

Through the floor — down to the roots! Don't betray
Your self, explore it to your worst feature!
Yours is theirs, brave girl, wise woman, teacher!

iii.

Desire is a prison, or a boudoir…
Where there is risk there's pleasure to be had.
Dare to transgress — bad is good, good is bad —
The degree depends only on how far.

How vigilant are these walls — How bizarre,
You're meant to fear your fantasies — How sad,
You can't touch yourself — it makes them so mad —
It's because — intimately, from afar —

You're touching them… Stand up! It's your body!
Rub your ass on those walls, your breasts, then tear
Out your heart from your chest, and press it there —

Then become them, dripping with blood, bawdy —
Now, one with your desire, invite *him* in —
You've discovered a room he's never been

In…

II

Subject to the patriarchy's desire,
I loved it, but in the most honest way…
The truth hurts, the fruit's bitter, and the prey
Is oftentimes yourself when the entire

Tree is a toxic and deluded liar —
Morals turn when history has its day,
Sermons smell off, the powerful decay
Of worldviews can make one sick — I aspire

To that bonfire on the horizon — Fell
This tragic trunk, toss it on — Hot as hell,
My branches and bark like incense will smoke.

Hypocrites and cowards, our pyre awaits!
Embody your desire, embrace your fates!
When the end's this clear, the rest is a joke.

III

They act as though nature's been aborted
By me, when he was all up in my womb —
He gets his kingdom — Me? This living tomb.
All because nature somehow got thwarted

By little old me — As if I courted
Father by choice — There I am at my loom,
A perfume wafts in, it pervades the room,
Something sensual with something sordid…

I look up from my shuttle, close my eyes…
And when I open them, what do I see?
His face in *my* weaving, staring at me —

Who seduced whom? Who offered prayers? Whose
prize
Was it to have the course reversed? Not mine!
I can't affect nature! Or things divine!

IV

Adonis

They sawed it out of me with the gods' help,
But fuck that child, it wasn't about that —
"Just take it! — the hypocrite's little whelp!
"Expose it! Use it! I don't care!" I spat.

"He wasn't trying to get me with child!"
They're all such liars — That's not why we fuck!
That's not why, me down on my knees, he smiled
When I took him in and started to suck!

No, he was not thinking of children then…
So, why do they — fucking — pretend to care?
Men don't rear us — Maybe then I'd have been
Less likely to love him that way… I bare

The blame, but get lauded for what I bore
Like a gem in the mud of a soiled whore —

Iphigenia, Jephthah's Daughter, Etc.

The shape of the world's the shape of my mind,
The shape of your eyes, my field of vision.
When you leave, I wait—but sometimes I find
I can't, and in moments of decision

I follow—or try to keep up behind
Your back turned, your lack of supervision;
Unseen in your shadow, your stark and blind
Resolve—lost in my tragic excision

From the horizon as seen in your eyes...
Should I blame the war, or should I blame you?
What or who has brought about my demise?

My future's in question—or is it through?
Your duty has come at too high a price,
Your glory to the gods, your sacrifice...

The Rape of Medusa

The victim-visions of men torment me.
One comes and is left, a look on his face
That speaks — like a mirror — of the disgrace,
Of the monster he saw and now I see.

I don't look out the windows at the sea —
The sound is enough to make my heart race —
I remember the smell, it filled the space —
He was wet when he held me down — when he —

I looked on — out of body — from above,
And wondered if this was what they called love...
The priestess's cries didn't seem to reach

The finned ears of the god. His eyes were green,
Coated with a film where she went unseen...
Lost to god and man, a monster to each.

Fallen Woman, *after Camille Thierry*

When I was fifteen, still pure, still indoors,
    I'd sing my songs at home
And when I got bored and finished my chores
    I'd go outside to roam

I'd bathe in the sound, the masculine whir
    Cicadas made resound;
And weighed down sometimes, in a humid blur
    I'd lay down on the ground

A handsome young man once brought words of fire
    And spoke them at my feet
He wanted me to combust with desire
    And fuel his with my heat

My body was clothed in a silky dress —
    His words were true in part;
Beneath words of love he hid more and less
    (Scorn, in place of a heart)

Dishonored and disappointed, I cried
    Ignored by him, alone
But where other girls might have swooned or died
    A pride inside me shone

I was still beautiful, still unfulfilled
    In life and in my dreams
At the word "convent" I laughed till I trilled —

Well, such is life it seems...

When I was fifteen, still pure, still indoors
I'd sing my songs at home
But when I got bored and finished my chores
I'd go outside to roam

To Corinne, *after Alexandre Latil*

Unhappy love is still above sadness.
                              Mme Desbordes Valmore

I must run from you, seductive Corinne —
Flee, never see you again, never be
Caught by your godlike attractiveness — screen
You out — do what I have to — you plague me…

Your eyes, when I saw them, were so direct,
Your features so charming, your smile so free;
Your voice, so soft, made my reason suspect,
And ever since, you've so tormented me…

Yes, it's done, your cherished image resides
Inside my heart, like a queen, where it reigns…
I could rebel, or join the suicides…
My life is now just the pain it contains…

Felicity, phantom ephemera!
In vain, my heart leaps grasping at its feet!
Not you too — don't be a vain chimera
Amused when I fail…to speak when we meet…

Not see you again? No! Who could subscribe
To that? Never hear your voice again… No!
I can love you, never tell you, describe
You in verse…and someday…maybe you'll know…

A Daydream

I read an anecdote about a breast[2]
Falling out of a dress—I did my best
To ignore it, but she caught me looking.
She fixed her boob, unhooking, rehooking,
Chasing my eyes like Diana mid-stalk.
She crossed the bar—towards me—I turned to walk—
And, just drunk enough to challenge the creep,
Said, "Wanna dance, or you just gonna peep?"
At that point my thoughts had wings and I said,
"Beauty slipping the straps," (I touched my head)
"Of life's fashion. I'm not drunk enough, but
If you take the lead…" —"Well, I tell you what…"
Then out on the street (we each took a drink)
We mississippied up Bourbon. The stink
Was familiar to us, like river mud
To a captain navigating the flood
Upriver when it rains. "Think it'll rain?"
I asked. —"It's gonna pour—blood and champagne!
Tonight's the decadent end to our days!
It's Babylon on Bourbon in a blaze!
The Théâtre de l'Opéra aflame!
The great deluge, but Noah's ark's old frame
Has not been maintained! The levees are cracked—
We're cracked—and—" I took her hand and we backed
Into the shadows of an ally. —"Let's

---

[2] In Ian McNulty's Katrina memoir *A Season of Night*.

Never come to…" — "Let's drown, caught in their
nets — "
"There's a chance we'll slip free…" — "Why bother
when
We are all doomed never to see again
The sun rise at the Mississippi's bend — "
Eyes closed, lips pursed…my dream came to an end.
I closed the book I'd been unreading, sighed —
I named her Nola in my mind and tried
To recall her…but there was no one there
On my dream Bourbon Street or…I don't know

where…

A Phantom, *after Baudelaire*

I. Shadows

Deep in the caves of an unending grief,
Where Destiny's already dismissed me —
Where there's no light to find, no colors see,
Just mourning, hosted by Night, no relief,

I'm like a painter, an unholy joke,
Painting in shadows black layer upon black
Or a chef whose dark tastes lead him to hack
Out his own heart, boil, and eat it like yolk,

But sometimes, here, there shines, stretches out,
sprawls
A spectre, in shape pure splendor and grace —
And like an exotic dream, it enthralls

Me, but when I look at it in the face…
How could I not know my beautiful guest!
Black yet luminous, it's Her, manifest.

II. Perfume

Reader, tell me, have you ever breathed in
With intoxication and slow excess
The incense that dwells in a chapel's recess
Or the musk that secretes from its sachet's skin?

Impossible charm, magical egress!
To find in the present the once-had-been—
Such is the beloved's warm body when
Love plucks from memory an old caress...

From her hair, from her thick and heavy curls,
Living sachet, pungent censer at mass,
An odor, savage and feral, unfurls;

And through her velvet and satin clothes pass,
Like a fabric saturated with youth,
The accents of her fur, raw and uncouth—

III. The Frame

As a frame sometimes will add something more
To a work, famous though its brush may be,
Something, I don't know, strange, otherworldly,
By setting it off against nature's galore;

Jewels were like that for her, gold, metals, décor
Seemed just to fit her exquisite rarity,
Nothing could obscure her perfect clarity,
Spotlighted, she seemed, by the things she wore.

One even could say that she really thought
Herself to be loved by all things. She drowned
Her nude body, voluptuously caught,

In linen kisses, a satin embrace,
And every movement, demure or unbound,
Evidenced her playful monkeylike grace.

IV. The Portrait

Death and Disease have reduced to ashes
The fires that used to burn for us two —
What of your eyes, hot, tender, their lashes —
What of your lips, my heart's bliss, what of you —

What of your kisses, they were like a balm
Forced on me, like sun, beyond my control —
What's left — my soul is unquiet, uncalm —
Nothing — this sketch, in three shades of charcoal

That, like me, fades away in solitude,
And that hateful Time, its wings spread apart,
Flaps at everyday, destructive and rude…

Pitch black assassin of Life and of Art,
You'll never snuff her out! My memory
Protects her, my late pleasure, my glory!

Beauty, *after Baudelaire*

I am beauty, O Mortals, a dream in stone
And these breasts, that bruise you, all of you, in turn,
Were made for the poet, to make his love burn
Eternal, like matter, as mute and unknown.

I reign in the azure — unfathomed sphinx;
To the swan's pure white join an ice cold heart;
I hate movements that draw straight lines apart;
I cry *never*, and my eye never winks.

Poets, before my sublime attitudes,
Alike to the greatest masterpieces,
Will strive for me each in their solitudes;

And for their love, so it never ceases,
I have smooth mirrors that make all things shine:
Eyes, these large, clear, eternal eyes of mine!

A Carcass, *after Baudelaire*

Remember, my darling, that thing we saw
    That mild and beautiful morning?
Off the path, in the gravel — and us in awe —
    A carcass appeared without warning.

Its legs in the air, like a lady of pleasure —
    It was cooking, fluids oozing out —
Cynically, carelessly exposing her treasure:
    A putrid abdomen, spoiled throughout.

The sun was shining on the rotting mess
    As though it meant to reduce it down
To its elements, and in the process
    Unbind for Nature what Nature had bound.

And the sky looked upon this precious mass
    As though it were blooming like a flower.
The smell was so strong, we feared, on the grass
    We'd pass out or be overpowered!

The flies were swarming — its stomach so putrid —
    With maggots streaming forth in legions —
They were pouring out, a viscous black fluid,
    Moving the rags meant to clothe those regions.

It rose and fell, undulating like a wave,
    And coursing with little clicking sounds.
It was as though the corpse, full then concave,

Breathed through the vermin that littered the
ground.

And the music produced by this teeming world
    Was like running water or the breeze,
Or a winnower's grain when gently swirled
    By his fan and its rhythmic ease.

Its contours were fading like a dream,
    Like a light sketch that will not stay
On a forgotten canvass, but whose theme
    Will be done from memory anyway.

An anxious dog from behind some boulders
    Was watching us with impatient eyes
For a chance to retrieve from its picked over
shoulders
    The piece of flesh she'd dropped when
surprised.

— And yet, you will be like this rotting mass
    Like this terrible infection,
O light of my eyes, O sun on my darkness
    O Goddess of my affection!

Yes, you, O queen of the Graces,
    After receiving your last rites,
Beneath the grass and petalful faces
    Will decompose with your bones and their
mites.

Greet them for me, my lady, but let them know,
    The worms kiss-eating those lips of yours,
That I've kept the divine essence from the pit below
    Of all my since decomposed amours.

The Patriarch's Carcass

after Baudelaire's Une Charogne

Remember, my love, that carcass we found
    just off the path, without warning?
Sweet boy, I bet you'd meant that spot of ground
    for me that warm summer morning!

I might have been game, but that day I learned…
    But wait — more about that later!
Remember how the sun had cooked and burned
    it's skin? Remember the crater

Between its legs excreting larvae, or…
    birthing them — like nature coursing,
Like a fertile girl, with life from a core
    that's rotting, but also forcing

New life into the world! Its legs were spread —
    Remember the smell? — *Unnerving,*
Right? It had such power for something dead —
    A brown juice came out, preserving

All the maggots covered in putrid oil.
    I joked, and you almost fainted
When I pointed to a space in the soil,
    "Why don't *you two* get acquainted?"

Was it the reek though? or was it the womb
    that this fresh nature had chosen?
The Gay implication: *You? Its bridegroom?*
    that held you there as though frozen?

Because *that* carcass had once been a man
    though now it looked like a woman;
There was a breeze that gently, like a fan,
    raised the hairs off its abdomen.

And even though it was headless, its chest
    was intact and flat and hairy;
Scavengers had come and left us the rest
    to gawk and stare at and tarry.

I don't know about you, but what I saw
    there in the grass, dead and rotting,
Was the patriarchy *at last* withdraw
    with all its unconscious plotting.

And the sight of that dead patriarch splayed
    made me question *your* conniving
To get me behind those trees, to get laid —
    a plan now not worth reviving.

That Patriarch said, *Memento mori,*
    but also, *New worlds are forming.*
There's more than meets the eye, look behind the
    maggots in my carcass swarming.

We turned our backs and, regaining the path,
    felt our relationship changing;
But it's not just us, in his aftermath
    the whole world is rearranging —

Ode to his Mistress, *after Ronsard*

My love, let's go see if that rose
Ready this morning to disclose
Its red robe's secrets to the day
Has not lost by day's end its flush,
The folds of its red dress, the blush
That, like yours, gives itself away.

Ah! But look, in such short a space,
My love, she's, in this very place,
Seen her beauty to pieces fall!
Oh, Nature's cruel! A cruel mother!
One day's rose won't see another,
And that one day's space is so small!

And so, my love, listen to me:
While you still possess the beauty
Of life in its first freshest bloom,
Gather up the blossoms of youth!
Take from this rose this brutal truth,
That age your beauty too shall doom.

Song for my Hairy Girlfriend

You know what I love about you?
        It's true!
You shock in a bikini bathing suit –
It's not that your breasts are the perfect shape
And it's not your ass that leaves me agape
        Not your long legs – *it's the dispute*

        I see in their eyes, and the fear
                I can hear
In their sharp sighs and disapproving gasps –
Your unshaven legs are covered with hair
But that's not it, it's what's writhing out where
        It shouldn't – it's Medusa's asps

        Like an orgasm spilling out,
                Like a spout
Of anti-bourgeoisie punk invective
And not just from the front, it's from the back,
A sexy, hairy female ass attack.
        Their morals are ineffective

        Against what you and nature bring,
                And I sing,
This everchanging diverse sexy beast –
I mean the world, its beauty and its change,
All the real things that convention finds strange
        And that we *don't,* not in the least…

Song

I'm so jealous of my girlfriend's tattoos
    So close to her skin
    They could be a bruise
I'm so jealous of my girlfriend's tattoos

I'd be jealous of my girlfriend's bruise too
    If it were one, but
    It's just a tattoo
I'd be jealous of my girlfriend's bruise too

I don't care for my girlfriend's lingerie
    It doesn't enhance
    It gets in the way
I don't care for my girlfriend's lingerie

And when it's cold I don't like socks in bed
    I say, *Tuck your feet*
    Under me instead
No, when it's cold I don't like socks in bed

Cause I like her naked, I want her nude
    But it's wild how she's
    Completely tattooed
Cause I like her naked, I want her nude

I can kiss her breasts, I can still go down
    Though her skin is inked
    Black, green, reddish brown

I can kiss her breasts, I can still go down

Even though in a sense she's clothed in ink
        It doesn't frustrate
        My nudity kink
Even though in a sense she's clothed in ink

But when she's clothed, I can't stop thinking of
        Her naked body —
        Yes, but then above
        All *those tattoos* un-
        Fitting like a glove,
        All those tattoos like
        A form of self-love —

I'm so jealous of
                my girlfriend's tattoos

Ekphrasis on the Sole of a Foot

The sole of my foot is like a cat's tongue.

I know — what you expect of me is smooth —
The soft, the velvet, but let's get real — I'm
Rough, with bits of hardness, parts of me scour
Things — like the walls of your heart — that's why I'm
Great, and desired — more naked than porn — I'm
My sole — here for you to kiss and devour
With the tender side of your face and lips.

Trust me, I want you like a lion's tongue.

Start with the extremity — when you're done,
Subject and one with the chafe of my foot,
Raw and needing a place to recover,
Find me — the rest of me's here, uncovered —

The rest of me's here to be discovered —

My Muse's Orgasm

When I told her *I came*

      exploding like a star,

She laughed, "Like a black hole,

      that's how I came, how far

"Inwards I lost myself,

      how hard I came apart.

"One with the undone, I

      became a work of art,

"Transfixing my own eyes

      on a multiple me,

"Captivated by be-

      ing both captive and free,

"Out of body because

      in it so completely,

"In silence screaming, re-

      fraining indiscreetly,

"Making no sound and yet

      I was not holding back.

"Your star danced around and

was swallowed by the black.

"This time, my poet, you

came, but I transcended.

"Naturally, my being

from the gods descended."

Overjoyed, I cried, "My

muse! My inspiration!"

And took her orgasm

for my next creation.

About the Author

Michael Perret is a poet and translator from Austin, Texas. He also fronts the French language noise pop duo Marking & Plating.

Also By Michael Perret

The Chimera and Other Dark Poems

Translation:
Octavia, the Quadroon, by Sidonie De La Houssaye